PRACTICE MAKES PROFIT

THE SMALL BUSINESS OWNER'S GUIDE TO MAKING MORE MONEY BY NOT WORKING HARDER

GRAHAM W. SCOTT

For James, who set me on the TOC path

CONTENTS

ISBN: 978-0-473-60755-5 (paperback)

ISBN: 978-0-473-60756-2 (Kindle)

This is a *not* a work of fiction. The successes achieved by the individuals in this book are accurate. However, to protect privacy, all names, as well as the details about the main character's medical specialization, have been changed.

Cover design by Olga Vynnychenko

Copyedited by Vesna Mirosavljev

Stock images used: (1) Vector: "A hand with a scalpel buts a dollar sign on skin," by crystaleyemedia on Depositphotos (https://depositphotos.com/108869988/stock-illustration-hospital-bills-or-medical-insurance.html), standard royalty-free license; (2) Vector: dollar bills by Mohamed Hassan on Pixabay (https://pixabay.com/vectors/money-plant-investment-cash-tree-6626359/); (3) Photo: "Neutral beige background, linen texture," by Annie Spratt on Unsplash (https://unsplash.com/photos/xTaOPMa6wAE).

Graham W. Scott

website: www.grahamwscott.com

email: graham@grahamwscott.com

INTRODUCTION

WHY ANOTHER BUSINESS BOOK?

This is a story about bottlenecks. More specifically, business bottlenecks.

It's based on the idea that every business has a chokepoint, a rate-limiting step or a bottleneck that caps its output.

If this wasn't the case, every business would just keep growing exponentially and they'd all be bigger than Microsoft. And we know that's not happening!

And yet most business owners have never thought about their business as having a bottleneck.

That's great news!

Why?

Because this means that as a business owner, you can harvest some low-hanging fruit at very little extra cost.

In fact that's exactly what happened to this one business owner I know, David.

David found his bottleneck and focused on it. He made sure it was working at full capacity. Then he maximized the revenue from that capacity, while changing the rest of the business so that it supported the bottleneck.

The business decisions (and this book!) were inspired by Eli Goldratt's famous book *The Goal* and the principles inside it. *The Goal* is set in a factory where the NCX-10 piece of machinery is the bottleneck. But I've discovered that the same bottleneck principle applies in all organizations that have limited resources, including not-for-profits.

The steps I used to guide David along are based on the Five Focussing Steps formalized by the Theory of Constraints International Certification Organization. However, I've chosen my friend Clarke Ching's easy-to-remember version of these steps, called FOCCCUS (or FOCUS). It stands for Find, Optimize, Coordinate, Collaborate, Curate, Upgrade and Start again.

This book covers F, O and the three Cs (with the option of obtaining the rest on my website for free).

In our story here you'll quickly learn that in service industries the bottleneck is a skilled person—in our case, a highly trained surgeon.

You can take the practical lessons in this book and apply them to any small businesses, service-based businesses or solopreneurial venture.

In this book you'll learn

1. why the money you spend on business improvements never seems to change the bottom line,
2. why small business owners get stuck in a holding pattern,
3. some practical ways to use the Theory of Constraints and
4. how to apply TOC to small business.

It's not a silver bullet; it does require hard work. But if you're working hard anyway, you might as well be working on the right things.

PART I

FIND

What (or Who) Is the Bottleneck?

1

YOU'RE NOT MAKING THE MONEY YOU SHOULD BE

David was keen to catch up over coffee.

He's a medical specialist and a very clever guy. As a dermatologist, he worked with the biggest organ in the human body and was trained to treat over 3,000 different skin conditions.

A typical day for David might involve diagnosing and prescribing drugs to treat infections, diagnosing and removing cancerous growths and treating chronic allergies.

To become a dermatologist, he had to first become a full medical doctor and then specialize. (We've joked about it taking six months to learn how to diagnose or cut someone up and sew them back together, and another 10 years to know what to do when it goes wrong!)

After all that training David was in his mid-30s when he got his first decent-paying job. He worked part-time at the local hospital and, at the same time, worked on getting his own private practice underway.

But get this.

In all those years he spent in medical school, the curriculum never included any business or financial training.

Nuts, if you ask me.

No wonder David was getting frustrated by the lack of progress with his finances a couple of years into his professional practice.

Most of his friends who'd left or finished school early to become plumbers and builders were nearly 20 years ahead of him on the property and retirement ladder. Plus they didn't carry the risk of medical malpractice, burnout and having their entire livelihoods depend on a steady hand and laser-sharp eyes. David desperately wanted to get a return on all the time he had invested in training just in case his body gave out.

"I just don't seem to be making the money I should be," David said to me. "My business expenses must be too high. My biggest cost is staff, so I'm wondering, *Have I got too many?!*"

I don't blame David for that logic. Accountants are great at looking to increase profits by cutting costs, and unfortunately this way of thinking has made its way into a lot of businesses.

But there's a problem with cutting costs: *you can only cut so much fat before you hit flesh.*

2

MAKE THE OLD CAR GO FASTER

David's a bit of a petrolhead, so I used my favorite car analogy on him. "If you wanted to make an old car go faster, where you would start?" I asked.

"You'd want to start in the place that will have the most impact. Which is likely to be the engine!" he responded confidently.

"So you wouldn't start stripping parts out to make it lighter?" I said, testing him.

"Cutting weight off it might make it go faster. But that's going to have a small effect and is probably one of the last things you'd do. You'd want everything else running properly first, and so you'd probably start by looking at the engine."

"And you wouldn't put in a new radio, then?" I asked.

"How on earth is that going to help? Adding something that doesn't help the engine won't make the car go faster!" he replied.

I told you he was clever!

"So it sounds like adding the wrong stuff or taking away things too early won't work," I said, awaiting his reaction.

"Absolutely," David said in agreement. "You need to look at where you can make the greatest difference."

3

BUT MY PRACTICE IS DIFFERENT!

"Have you ever heard of a way of thinking about business called the Theory of Constraints?" I asked. "In a nutshell, it's really just a fancy way of saying, 'Focus on the business bottleneck.'"

David looked a bit blank, so I grabbed a paper napkin and drew a quick diagram.

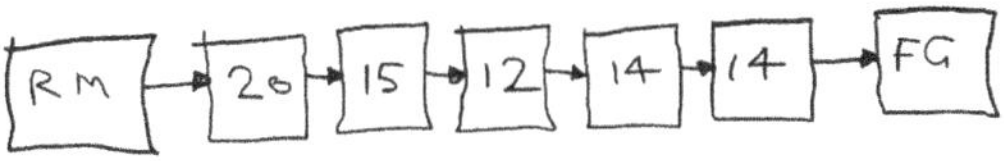

"So, David, imagine this is a simple factory, with raw materials getting fed into a chain of five machines and finished goods coming out the other end. Looking at this diagram, we can say that the number of units each machine can produce per hour is between 12 and 20. So what's the maximum number of units this whole system can produce in one hour?"

(By the way, I've had the odd person overcomplicate this

and start adding them all together, but David didn't make that mistake!)

"It's obvious that the factory can only produce a maximum of 12 units per hour because the third machine is the bottleneck." David paused for a moment and continued, "But even though this sounds good in theory, I'm running a medical practice—not a factory—so we're completely different!"

"I think you'd be surprised," I replied. "I used to think that my accounting practice was different until I realized that we take raw materials in the form of bank documents and invoices, and then put them through a series of processes until we come up with finished goods in the form of financial statements and income tax returns. Don't you take raw materials in the form of patients with problems, then put them through a series of processes to assess them, operate on them and fix their problems?"

"When you put it like that, I suppose yes, we do."

"Almost every system has a chokepoint. A factory, a medical practice, a restaurant. Even a traffic flow system like a motorway [or freeway, for you North American folk]. We know there are chokepoints there. Otherwise we'd have infinite capacity and never have traffic jams."

"I suppose it's a bit like the 'rate-determining step' we learned about in Chemistry 101. The reaction can only go as fast as the slowest step," David chimed in.

"Exactly! And if the idea is to maximize the flow of work through an organization, you had better be maximizing the flow through the bottleneck. So, David, what's the bottleneck in your business?" I asked.

"Oh, we've got *lots* of those. Sometimes we don't have enough patients, sometimes we don't have enough instruments, sometimes it's the staff. I could go on," he said.

That wasn't a very useful answer.

Having lots of bottlenecks or having "wandering bottlenecks" is usually a sign that no one is even focusing on the bottleneck, let alone managing it.

At the end of the day in this type of simple business, there can be only one weakest link in the chain. Only one true bottleneck.

So it was time to replay one of David's stories back to him.

4

WANDERING BOTTLENECKS

"Did you know these 'wandering bottlenecks' are usually a sign that no one has thought about where the real bottleneck is?"

"What do you mean?" asked David.

"Do you remember the story you told me once about working at the hospital? How one of the board members was walking through and saw a couple of porters idly standing around having a chat? And how that led to some redundancies to save cost on excess porters?"

"Yes," replied David, rolling his eyes. "And then a couple of weeks later a surgery had to be canceled because there were no spare porters to bring the next patient to the team of surgeons and nurses who were scrubbed up and ready to go! The whole operating time was wasted."

"So, saving money in a relatively low-cost link in the chain caused it to become a bottleneck, while a highly trained, highly skilled and expensive medical team was unemployed?"

"Yes," he agreed, "and it makes me think the bottleneck

in the hospital is probably the operating theaters. Every canceled operation is time lost."

"Good point," I said. "That's one of the features of the true bottleneck. If you have idle time at the bottleneck, you've lost that capacity forever. And if you haven't identified your bottleneck, you could be losing lots of potential output! Sometimes the bottleneck is obvious. And sometimes it appears to be wandering—and in that case you have to make a call about where your bottleneck *should* be!"

I paused for a moment, watching the wheels turn, and then added, "You've said you have bottlenecks all over the place, David. Where do you think your bottleneck *should* be?" I asked.

(For you TOC diehards, the absolutely strategic leverage point is the constraint. Bottlenecks move!)*

"It should be me, shouldn't it?" said David, realizing he was the same as that team of surgeons in the hospital.

It seemed obvious now.

The business makes money only when David is consulting or on the end of a scalpel or laser. When he's idle, the business doesn't make money.

(By the way, this is typical of many medical and professional businesses. If you've ever wondered why your dentist seems expensive, it's because they're often the only person supporting a receptionist, a chairside assistant, as well as paying the rent, power, phone and all the insurances that go along with a professional practice!)

Once you start looking for it, your own bottleneck is usually easy to spot. Most of the time it's your most expensive resource. And that could be a piece of equipment, a person or group of people with similar skills.

Sometimes it's the resource with the most work piled up

in front of it waiting to be done. Or perhaps you'll spot idle people or machines downstream from the bottleneck.

Occasionally, the bottleneck seems to be outside the business. If your suppliers are your limiting factor, then you (or your procurement of people) need to talk to them or consider using different ones. If you have more product or more service capacity than market share, then the market is your bottleneck. (Or more precisely, your marketing department is the bottleneck, and you need to crank up your sales machine!)

~

*Note: In this book, for simplicity, I use the words *constraint* and *bottleneck* interchangeably.

PART II

OPTIMIZE

Fill the Capacity

5

DAVID'S FOUR HOURS

This might surprise you, but unless people are aware that a bottleneck exists, you can pretty well bet on it not being fully productive. It's rare for a bottleneck to be optimized when no one even recognizes that it's a bottleneck. In other words, managing bottlenecks requires being intentional about it.

This means the bottleneck will not be working 100% of the time it could on the correct type of work. A machine might be idle, or a highly skilled person might be doing a low-level task someone else should be doing. This is good news because with little or no investment, you can increase output significantly.

David and I returned to the car analogy for a bit.

"If you wanted to make that old car go faster, and you had decided the engine was the bottleneck, what would you do?" I asked.

"Probably start by making sure it was firing on all cylinders, fuel mix was right, air filter clean, all that sort of stuff, I suppose," David replied.

"So in other words, making sure it was running at full

capacity?"

"Exactly!"

"And are you running at full capacity?" I followed up.

I wanted to make sure David was on the end of a scalpel or laser and earning as much money as possible for the most amount of time possible.

First, we established that there were plenty of patients queueing up for procedures. We concluded that the market was *not* the bottleneck.

What complicated the situation was the need to have a specialist operating room that's fully equipped for day surgery cases. Operating rooms like these are shared with others and booked for four-hour time slots. So our first step was to make sure that the *whole* four hours of operating room time slots were being used.

David explained that making sure those four hours were consistently full wasn't quite that easy.

"We try to have our operating times reasonably well filled, but we need to leave some slots available for urgent treatment, such as a biopsy for a fast-growing skin cancer. And then of course some of our patients will have something important come up or get sick at the last minute and have to cancel or postpone."

David went on to say that despite there being plenty of patients requiring treatment, the staff were trained to be customer focused and scheduled appointments based on when it suited the patients.

This meant they would often open a new operating slot for bookings rather than fill each one completely first.

And this often resulted in partly filled operating time slots, which was worsened if an emergency slot went unfilled or patients canceled, further wasting potential scalpel time.

6

SWIM SCHOOL

I began to tell David about the work I had done with the local swim school. They operated under the umbrella of the local council-owned complex and were allocated pool space to teach children to swim.

Each half-hour lesson needed an instructor.

But here's the thing.

The cost of that instructor to the swim school was the same—regardless of whether one child enrolled or six.

And let's say a particular class only had a few enrolled, quite often the instructor would be paid to turn up only to find that all the kids in that small class were sick and/or had other commitments.

David quickly figured out the following three things:

1. The pool space was the bottleneck.
2. The first two kids covered the instructor's wages.
3. Only after that did the swim school have any income to cover administration, equipment and everything else.

When I first spoke to the swim school boss, the issue was that too many slots were being opened up and only partly filled.

David understood the scenario completely, and his first job was to go back and talk to the staff who were booking the surgical procedures. They needed to make sure they filled each new operating list before opening a new one, although they were still to leave a couple of strategic gaps for emergency work every week.

The simple act of filling the available bottleneck capacity was enough homework for this session, so David departed happily, and we agreed to meet again.

7

MAXIMIZING THE DOLLARS

To recap, once we had identified the bottleneck, our first job was to make sure that David's capacity was not being wasted.

Every blank slot in his operating lists was time (and money) that could never be recovered. So we had to make sure that there were enough patients there.

The lesson here is to first ensure the existing bottleneck capacity is full.

After all, until you're fully using what you've got, there's no point worrying about adding any more capacity to the system.

Now that the existing capacity was being fully utilized, it was time to make sure it was earning David the most money possible.

"How are the operating lists looking now?" I asked David when we met next.

"Full," he replied with a smile on his face.

"Good," I said. "Now we can have a talk about throughput velocity."

I received the blank look I was expecting.

"It's no good just being busy," I continued. "We need to measure the rate at which you're making money. Earning $10,000 a day is good; taking two months to earn it, not so good. If we've decided that it makes sense to focus on productivity through the bottleneck, then it also makes sense to focus our accounting measures on dollars through the bottleneck. Let me tell you about a couple of restaurants I've been to lately."

8

THE RESTAURANT THAT COULD HAVE DRAINED MY WALLET

A restaurant is also usually constrained by its floor area, which determines how many tables it can hold.

After I finished university, I got a job in Atlanta, Georgia, and one of the things we did almost daily was go out to lunch. We frequently went to a Chinese restaurant and would pay a few dollars for a meal. One day I was accidentally handed the evening menu. The food choices were identical, but the prices were three times as much. It dawned on me that the restaurant's earnings per table were the dollars per sitting, multiplied by the number of sittings per table.

At lunchtime the restaurant was focused on the number of sittings by turning the same table over three, four or five times. In the evening they could sell the tables only once or twice. And so they focused on the dollar amount per sitting by charging more for the food (and, no doubt, selling as many drinks as they possibly could!).

I was reminded of this 30 years later in New Zealand when a group of 10 of us went out to celebrate my son's 21st birthday. We arrived on time. After seating us and giving us water, the server disappeared. It was Friday night. The restaurant was not overly busy, and everyone was keen to have a drink and unwind.

After a 20-minute drought, I went searching for our server. (I should probably point out that we don't tip in New Zealand as a rule, so service is highly variable!) By the time she had taken our orders and brought the 10 drinks to the table, another 10 minutes had passed. Every time we needed a refill, we had to go and find a server and then wait for the bar staff to pour 10 drinks.

Apart from only getting nine main meals and having to wait for the last one, we ended up having a great night out and lovely food. However, by the time they offered us dessert—about three hours after we had arrived—no one was interested.

The point is that I had budgeted about $100 per head, but the bill worked out to less than $65 per head. I suspect the server was a student, worked only part-time and earned minimum wage. No one had spent the time to train her.

We were the only people who were using that table that night, and the staff should have been trying to maximize the money from that table. They could easily have emptied my wallet a further $350 by training someone to keep our drinks full and offer starters, coffee and liqueurs and generally pay more attention. And we would have been the happier for it.

9

THE RESTAURANT THAT DID

By coincidence, my brother was in town a few weeks later, and he was disappointed to have missed my son's celebration. So we put together a very similar group of 10 to go out dinner. But after our previous experience, we decided to go somewhere different.

I made a reservation for 6 p.m. and was warned there was another booking for the same table at 8 p.m. We arrived and I was greeted by name by our very attentive server, who then sat us down and immediately offered us drinks. We had a wonderful night, with starters, mains and desserts all around. Our beer and wine glasses were kept topped up, and we finished almost exactly at 8 p.m. without feeling rushed at all. The bill at the end of the night was $95 per head. An extra $300 painlessly extracted from my wallet.

The difference is even more impressive when we look at the rate at which the restaurants earned their money. Our previous experience netted the restaurant $650 over a three-hour period for that table—in other words, slightly under $220 per hour. The second restaurant made $950 over two hours, so $475 per hour.

If your tables are the bottleneck and the window for eating is that four-hour window between 6 and 10 p.m., then the first restaurant had limited themselves to one sitting and $650 for that table.

The second restaurant had sold the table a second time and had the potential to make the same amount again, thus getting $1,900 from the table for the night.

Obviously, this is not all profit. The cost of the food and drink is likely around 40%. The margin from the two tables at the two different restaurants might look something like this:

	Restaurant 1	Restaurant 2 (our sitting)	Restaurant 2 (2 sittings)
Table sale per night	$650	$950	$1,900
Cost of food/drink @40%	$260	$380	$760
Gross profit (throughput)	$390	$570	$1,140
Gross profit per hour	$130	$285	$285

If you take it to another level, it's even worse. If each table had to cover $300 a night in fixed costs like wages, rent, power, advertising, etc., then Restaurant 1 has made $90 and Restaurant 2 has made $840. The effect of more hours and more dollars per hour is massive.

When your bottleneck is the number of tables you have, then leaving that bottleneck to the mercy of underpaid, untrained staff is just plain crazy. The effect that the extra drinks and food sold has on the bottom line is well out of proportion to the extra few dollars per hour on the wage bill.

After telling David the whole story, I said, "And guess which restaurant we'll be going back to? I'll just have to make sure to book early!"

10

MAXING OUT THE HIGH-END WORK

"So, it's not just enough to have my lists full. I need to know how much each procedure is worth?" asked David.

"Yes, and how long it takes. We need to find out the rate at which you're earning money on a dollars-per-minute basis. That's your homework this time."

Making sure David's bottleneck capacity was fully utilized was a two-step process:

1. he first needed to make sure every minute of operating time was full, and
2. he had to make sure each of those minutes was worth the maximum number of dollars possible.

If we think back to the motorway/freeway chokepoint, we want to ensure traffic flow is optimized.

Too much traffic turns the freeway into a carpark (or parking lot, for you North American folk).

Too little traffic means we miss out on potential flow.

There is a sweet spot somewhere in the middle that maximizes flow.

While we can gauge the flow of traffic by looking or counting, if we install a modern electronic tollgate, we can measure the flow of money through the chokepoint. Since different vehicle types pay different tolls, we could adjust the prices we charge to further increase our revenue.

But unlike a freeway—where we can control prices but not the mix of vehicles—in business we can adjust not only the prices *but also the equivalent of "the mix of vehicles"* at the on-ramps. And by doing so, we can find that sweet spot that maximizes income through the proverbial tollgate.

The spreadsheet David sent through a couple of days later was enlightening for both of us. He had worked out the throughput of each type of procedure he did by taking the cost to the patient, less direct costs that were paid to outside parties (like operating room fees, anesthetics and consumables). He then divided that by the number of minutes it took him to operate.

The cheapest work involved minor skin lesion removal or freezing lesions with a CryoProbe, while high-end work including the use of collagen fillers and Botox injections earned four times as much on a per-minute basis.

Although he decided to increase some prices, the exercise highlighted the need to change the combination of procedures he was doing to increase the amount of high-end work.

Everything was beginning to head in the right direction, but David still needed a major shift in mindset.

11

BUT WHAT ABOUT THE COSTS?

Three weeks passed and David called me. He sounded confused, so we agreed to meet. When we did, I discovered he was still worrying about costs and wanted to do some budgeting.

Although he understood that he needed to concentrate on the flow of dollars through the bottleneck, he was still a bit fixated on the costs and figured they should be budgeting in some form or another. After all, even though our focus was on dollars through the bottleneck, we obviously couldn't afford to ignore fixed costs like rent, power and wages! So we worked out some targets that he and his staff would have to meet.

In my experience, many business owners don't really understand budgets, so it's unrealistic to expect their staff to comprehend them. I've found the simplest way to deal with this is to work out their total annual expenses on a daily or perhaps weekly basis.

In my accounting practice we worked out our fixed costs for the year and then divided that by the number of days per year we were open. That showed us in a simple way that we needed to be invoicing just over $5,000 per day to cover our costs. This served two purposes:

1. It gave us a benchmark for our costs, which we could monitor and react accordingly if it began to rise.
2. It gave us a figure to focus on beating with our daily output. And having that knowledge was the real benefit.

I went through the same exercise with another client. She had a retail shop and was trying to hand the day-to-day operations over to her staff. She came in to see me about setting a budget for them.

Rather than train her staff to read and react to budgets, we worked out a fixed cost figure of about $1,000 per day. That meant that at an average 40% gross margin, they just had to focus on selling more than $2,500 per day.

She gave her staff the freedom to get on social media, pay for Google ads and pull whatever levers they needed to ensure they hit that target. Simple but effective.

David and I went through the "daily cost" exercise. He soon realized that if "David the bottleneck" was at full capacity, and that capacity was maximizing income, then costs just weren't a problem any longer.

PART III

COORDINATE, COLLABORATE, CURATE

Make the Bottleneck King!

12

GETTING A RELIABLE OUTCOME

Even though focusing on costs became less important, David needed to coordinate all parts of the business to maintain good flow through the system so the bottleneck was fully utilized.

It was essential he didn't pull a "hospital porter" scenario we mentioned earlier and have this hard work sabotaged by lack of resources around him. We had to have buffers in place to protect the bottleneck's capacity.

I'm sure you'd agree we're all subject to variability and unpredictability in various areas of our lives. But have you ever thought about the huge resources that go into trying to predict and eliminate or dampen the effects?

A large multinational company might have the clout to force their suppliers or customers to absorb the variability.

For the rest of us, what really matters is that we get a reliable outcome.

Rather than trying to reduce or remove unpredictability, adding in a buffer means we can have a reliable outcome.

Unpredictability + Buffer = Reliable Outcome

13

BUFFERS

Most of us use buffers in everyday life without even thinking about it.

My wife is English and occasionally flies from New Zealand to the United Kingdom to visit her family. My job is to pick her up from the airport when she flies home.

Door to door, her trip is at least 36 hours. That's enough to make anyone grumpy! If I'm late to pick her up or if there are delays on our way home, I know I'm going to be in trouble.

If I get a really clean run, it takes me just under two hours to get to the airport. Depending on the time of day, I need to allow for traffic. Given how long my wife's flight is, it's not uncommon for the plane to catch jet streams and arrive up to 40 minutes early. So I usually leave about three or three-and-a-half hours before the scheduled landing time. This gives me enough time to absorb that variability and make sure I'm there waiting at the arrivals lounge.

I have a time buffer.

One time when I went to the airport, I struggled to get

my credit card to work in the very user-unfriendly pay-parking machines. So now I prefer to use cash.

And because I don't know how long I'll be waiting and how big the bill will be, I always have plenty.

I have a cash buffer.

When leaving the airport with my wife, I also want to drive home without having to stop. That means I must allow for extra fuel being burned while stuck in traffic, so I always leave home with a full tank of gas.

I have a resources buffer.

These types of buffers are the secret to absorbing the variability and keeping your bottleneck busy!

But back to David.

Our next job was to make sure David had the right buffers in place to facilitate a coordinated flow of patients through his business.

14

ROCKS, PEBBLES, SAND

In a previous conversation David had said that it was difficult to keep the operating lists at full capacity because he needed to (1) keep some space available for emergencies and (2) allow for last-minute patient cancelations.

Plus, the procedures took varying amounts of time. This variability meant that valuable capacity was being lost ... permanently.

He needed some buffers.

"I've come across this sort of problem before," I said. "One of the things businesses often do is treat all work as if it's the same, especially when it comes to scheduling."

I remembered a familiar metaphor.

"I'm sure you've heard the story about the college professor who filled a large jar to the brim with rocks and asked his class if it was full. He then added pebbles and sand."

"Familiar with that one," said David. "And the moral of the story is don't do all the small jobs first, because there won't be enough room for the big ones. That's all fine and well, but it doesn't help me fit in emergency pebbles or replace rocks that don't turn up for appointments."

"I had a client a few years ago who had a specialist diesel/truck workshop. Their job was to keep expensive machinery working by maintaining it and fixing it when it broke down. In most cases the owners of the machinery would have taken out big finance loans. Trucks don't make money when they're off the road, so there's real pressure to get the workshop maintenance work done quickly as well as respond to breakdowns out on the road."

"You mean dealing with emergencies like I sometimes do?"

"Exactly! And the bottleneck was the three mechanics who did all the maintenance and breakdown work. They had plenty of work, but the workshop itself was disorganized. So although the mechanics were busy, their time was not used effectively. For instance, they tended to be quiet on a Monday, but by the end of the week they were up to their necks and often had to work all weekend to catch up—all on overtime.

"After agreeing where the bottleneck was, the next step was to make sure the three mechanics' capacity of 8 hours a day each (for a total capacity of 24 overlapping hours a day) was put to full use. It turned out that the jobs varied both in terms of how they long took and how urgent they were.

"Big jobs would tie up the mechanics, so the small stuff wasn't getting done. And if they did all the small jobs, the big jobs would drag out for weeks. Emergency breakdown work was obviously high priority, but often a farmer would drop off a tractor or bulldozer and not need it for several weeks.

"We had a look through the previous three years' jobs to

get a feel for the pattern of work. Then we categorized the jobs the way we would rocks/pebbles/sand:

- Jobs expected to take less than 3 hours
- Jobs expected to take 3 to 6 hours
- Jobs expected to take more than 6 hours
- Jobs were also categorized into urgent and non-urgent jobs

"We then put rules in place:

- No more than one 6+ hour job scheduled for the day
- No more than 70% of capacity was scheduled for the day (to leave room for emergencies)
- If the time set aside for emergency work was not needed, pull forward the most urgent work
- If the time set aside for emergency work was insufficient, push back some non-urgent work

"The jobs for the week were put on a big board that was visible to everyone. At the beginning of the week, the boss could see if there were any holes. He would fill them by spending 15 to 20 minutes on the phone with his customers to see who needed any work done."

Pensive, David nodded and said, "I think we do an informal 'rocks/pebbles/sand thing' to make sure each list has a mixture, but it certainly wouldn't do any harm to have some simple rules for the receptionist. And it has always made sense to leave some slots open for emergencies, but I don't need to allow as much as your mechanic.

"The bit I'm struggling with is how I could pull work forward like he does. It can be a real hassle for our patients to rearrange things. Most of them have to arrange leave from work, sometimes childcare, someone to drive them and all those sorts of things."

"Most of them?" I asked.

He took a moment to think about it. "Well, I suppose there might be some who are self-employed or retired who might be able to come at a moment's notice."

"And would they benefit from jumping to the front of the line?"

"Absolutely! You should hear the moans when they realize they have to wait four to six weeks for the operation! I guess I assumed that no one could come at short notice. I might still be right, but it's certainly worth testing."

David went back to the practice and added a question to his initial patient consultation form asking if they'd be available to come at short notice. It turned out that a good number of his patients said yes, which meant he now always had a list of "stand-by" patients to fill last-minute empty slots.

This "short notice" list is activated when patients who are contacted a couple of days before their operation are now no longer available. This effectively gives David a time buffer. He has enough patients in reserve to cover any potential time losses.

15

RESOURCE BUFFERS

We'd made a great start by identifying David as the bottleneck and making sure his operating capacity was as full as possible.

The next step was to protect this new way of working.

We needed to build protective capacity around him, so that David never stopped working on account of a less essential resource's inability to keep up with him. This was key to stopping the "wandering bottleneck" syndrome that most businesses keep dealing with. We didn't want another resource unintentionally becoming the bottleneck!

When we began the exercise, David's target was to do four medical procedures in the four-hour time slot, with the aim of making an average throughput of $1,000 per procedure.

To uncover the pieces of the puzzle (i.e., the supposed wandering bottlenecks), I asked him a question: "What's stopping you from doing five procedures during the operating time?"

We quickly established that it wasn't David's fatigue levels. He loved operating. And when he was in "the zone," time flew. And mentally, he could easily cope with an extra procedure in four-plus hours of continuous operating.

It turned out that the first real problem was that when a procedure went quickly, the time saved was usually lost because the next set of instruments required were still in the sterilizer.

It took an hour to properly sterilize instruments between operations, and if an operation finished in under 60 minutes, the second set of instruments would not be ready for the next patient. The time saved by finishing quickly was being wasted.

16

THE MASSAGE THERAPIST

"David, let me tell you about my massage therapist, Katelyn. I went for a massage last week and was talking to Katelyn as she worked her magic on my back and shoulders. She charges $55 for an hour in her studio and has just started offering corporate massages at client offices. She takes a special chair with her that people can sit in and lean forward so it cradles their head, neck, shoulders and back.

"Katelyn thought that charging a dollar a minute was reasonable and that 15 minutes per massage was too short, but 20 minutes would be long enough for people to get the benefit without taking too much time out of their workday. But there were a few problems.

"For one, at the end of the massage when the person was fully relaxed, it wasn't exactly easy to get them off the chair quickly without undoing a lot of the good stuff! It would also take a few moments to wipe down the chair and for the new person to settle in before she could start again.

"She told me her aim was to give two massages per hour at $20 each, which meant she was going to earn $15 less than she would normally make in an hour and $20 less than she could potentially make by charging out 60 minutes every hour. Bear in mind that doesn't even account for her travel time.

"Sometimes Katelyn was the bottleneck, but at other times she was allowing the chair to become the bottleneck. This was effectively cutting down her earning potential by 33%. Sometimes we need to think strategically about where the real bottleneck should be. I'm an accountant and I've always said that without the numbers you're just guessing. After Katelyn had explained her new venture, my first question was about numbers.

"'How much does a chair cost?' I asked her. It turned out that for $450, Katelyn could get another chair. While she finished one massage, the next customer could be getting themselves ready. And the person who'd just received a massage could feel free to relax there for a bit and gradually get themselves ready to return to work. Getting an extra chair turned out to be a no-brainer.

"Now those extra few minutes of relaxation feel like part of the service, add value and don't even take up Katelyn's time. The new chair will have a payback of under 30 hours and will last for years.

"The whole point of the story here is that the bottleneck should never be limited by a non-bottleneck! It's *perfectly acceptable* for the second massage chair to be empty. What's not acceptable is for Katelyn to be idle because she doesn't have a chair available."

17

DAVID'S INSTRUMENTS

I let the story sink in for a moment.

"How much would a third set of instruments cost?" I asked David.

"They're quite expensive," he said. "About three grand."

I waited while he did the math in his head. We certainly didn't need a calculator to realize that the cost of a third set of instruments would be recovered from three extra procedures and that purchasing an additional set was a no-brainer.

"I guess I'd better buy another set of instruments," David said.

"Good thinking. Now what else holds you up?" I asked.

"Sometimes I get so busy that the surgical nurses can't keep up and I'm kept waiting."

Out came the calculator again. Not surprisingly, the cost of employing an extra nurse was a fraction of the income he'd be making from an extra procedure. It made economic sense to hire an extra one for the operating time.

I sensed some resistance.

"But they'll be sitting round with nothing to do half the time!" said David.

"So what?" was my deep and meaningful reply as I slipped into silence and gave him some space to think it through.

"I suppose it would be good for them to have a chance to rest. A four-hour session can be hard work for them," said David.

But he didn't sound completely convinced.

It's strange. A farmer can be quite happy having a $200K tractor sitting around doing nothing. But the idea of having a $30–50K worker left occasionally idle is completely unacceptable. It's such a foreign concept to most people and yet so vital to having an efficient bottleneck. And this next step was important enough that I decided we'd need to revisit it next time.

It was time to tell David about Jeremy.

18

IDLE PEOPLE

Jeremy was a senior developer/team lead at a software company. He came to one of the Black Belt in Thinking courses I facilitate, absolutely convinced that the people on his team were incompetent idiots. The team just wasn't getting through all their work. And as the leader, he was so busy that he knew his only option was to hire more staff.

Over the years I'd had a few clients complain about their staff, so after listening to Jeremy let off steam for a while, I asked him point-blank, "Why are you hiring idiots?"

Jeremy's immediate response was that of course he wasn't hiring idiots.

"So what do you do to turn them into idiots, then?"

By the end of his three-day analysis, he had come to the realization that the reason he was overworked was because he had hired too many new staff ... and that hiring even more would make the whole thing much, much worse. The new staff would need training, which would take him away from his main task.

He also realized he had inadvertently taught his existing

staff that he'd fix all their coding mistakes for them. Any issues they had were being "reverse delegated" and ended up in his in-tray.

It was like having every on-ramp feeding into the chokepoint at full capacity. As we've already established, a fully used freeway or motorway is called a carpark!

It turned out that a major issue was that instead of planning their coding work properly, Jeremy's staff were "saving time" by just getting stuck into it. They were making mistakes and then bringing them to Jeremy.

Not wanting them to be idle, Jeremy would send them off to attend to other matters while he tediously fixed their mistakes. But all he ended up doing was reinforce the "non-planning" behavior.

This is an excellent example of "efficiency" thinking in the wrong place causing more harm than good!

If Jeremy can fix something in an hour that takes a junior developer four hours to fix, then it's more "efficient" for Jeremy to do it. But the negative side effect of this thinking is that it takes Jeremy away from important bottleneck work. Worse yet, it frees up the junior to cause another hour of mayhem!

Jeremy didn't understand protective capacity yet.

And all his staff were painfully aware of this unwritten rule: if you're idle, you get fired.

This meant Jeremy's staff were constantly looking around for work and often dragging non-urgent future work forward. And when they got stuck, Jeremy felt obliged to drop his urgent work to help them so they could remain "productive." Ironically, having everyone productive was causing Jeremy, and therefore the whole team, to become unproductive.

He came to realize that he had to permit his staff to be

idle. The new objective was to have the bottleneck—Jeremy—*working on the right stuff* as much as possible, even if it meant a junior developer taking four hours to so something he could do in an hour!

Jeremy also realized that by fixing their problems for them, he had been robbing his staff of an opportunity to learn and grow. (Funnily enough, while Jeremy was away on the course, the team had to fix their own problems, and their output and productivity improved!)

19

PROTECTIVE CAPACITY AROUND THE BOTTLENECK

I finished off by going back to our car analogy.

"Think of your theater staff a bit like Lewis Hamilton's Formula 1 pit crew. Their job is to make sure he's off the track for the absolute minimum amount of time. The only way they can do that is by being idle! It's the only way they'll be ready to go the precise moment he enters the pit lane. Imagine if the pit crew manager didn't like idle people and sent them off to clean the toilets or pick up supplies at the wrong time."

David replied with a medical analogy. "Yes, I can see it's the same as the ambulance service; we definitely don't want 100% utilization. I need to be comfortable enough with this to give my people permission to be idle."

It had taken a while to get David on board with the idea of having idle staff. The concept seems counterintuitive at first, especially since we've been putting productivity on a pedestal for years. But David saw the common sense in it now and was ready to take it to another level again.

He understood now that having someone else idle was perfectly acceptable as long as *he* was busy. In fact, what was completely unacceptable was for *him* to be idle on account of his staff's inability to keep up!

And as it turned out, the nurses were grateful to have the odd break after being on their feet for four hours.

The whole point was to eliminate anything that could possibly interfere with David's ability to be 100% flat-out operating during those four-hour operating sessions.

This is an important step people often miss.

In David's case, once we pointed out that David himself was the bottleneck, we needed to have excess, protective capacity around him. Without this, David was under the impression that he had lots of bottlenecks or "wandering bottlenecks" moving around the business. Lack of instruments, not enough nurses. In reality, there should be only one weakest link in the chain.

But as is often the case, we get sidetracked and sucked into chasing efficiency, and we forget that the primary focus is to maximize the flow of work and dollars through the bottleneck. There is no surer way to decrease that flow than having non-bottlenecks efficiently running at full capacity.

What we really want is the bottleneck being efficient and the non-bottlenecks being effective. And being effective means keeping the bottlenecks efficient, which can sometimes mean being idle.

But I wasn't quite finished.

We needed to cover anything else that was putting David's bottleneck capacity at risk.

20

WHAT COULD POSSIBLY GO WRONG?

It now seemed so intuitive to have protective capacity in the form of extra instruments and nurses.

Since we'd been talking about turning around used instruments, I asked, "What's the state of the autoclave sterilizing equipment?"

"It's getting tired, but it's still working OK," said David.

I thought of a chat I'd had recently with a colleague who was doing some work with a gardening center. The owner had realized that the bottleneck of his business was the shop counter he sold most of his stock through. So when the local power company said there was a problem with the local electricity supply and they couldn't guarantee the power to his sales computer and payment system for the next three months, it made absolute sense for him to protect his bottleneck by investing in his own diesel power generator.

So I asked David, "What happens if your autoclave fails during an operating session?"

"Apart from losing the income from the rest of the operations that day, there is all the hassle of rebooking everyone when the upcoming lists are full."

We quickly agreed that updating the autoclaves was actually a cheap form of insurance!

We had come a long way from our original conversation where David's solution to low profits was to cut costs, probably by reducing staff. Following our conversations, he purchased instruments and autoclaves and was prepared to spend money on more nursing resources.

It was now time for David to make sure that the extra investment wouldn't be wasted because he ran out of work.

He needed to optimize the flow of patients through the practice.

21

FEEDING BUFFER

Patients are referred by their GP and then meet with David for a consultation to decide what the next steps are. A reasonable number need to have operations, so these sessions are a way to create a buffer of patients that feed directly into David's operating lists.

However, when I next caught up with David, he sounded a bit alarmed. Now that he was using his operating capacity better, he was starting to run out of patients. The buffer was emptying faster than he could refill it, and whenever it got too small, he would start to have idle time during his operating lists.

I've come across this issue before, so I told David about a client who was a kitchen manufacturer. This client's business went through two or three of its own little boom-and-bust cycles all within the same financial year. The problem was they would have a blitz on marketing and create a big wave of forward work. But then they'd get so busy they would stop marketing for some time.

When the busy period was over, suddenly there'd be

nothing to do, and the company would launch a frantic effort to secure work of any sort to keep the doors open.

This rollercoaster ride between production and marketing caused all sorts of knock-on effects. Cash flow was all over the place. The workshop went from empty to being so full of work that no one could find anything, which in turn caused delays and upset customers.

Rather than cycling between extremes, it made sense for them to have a continuous but moderate level of work in front of them. They needed to create a feeding buffer of incoming work.

We analyzed their process from initial contact right through to securing the work. From the first point of contact to preparing the quote, having it accepted and then starting to build the new kitchen, my client's process averaged about three months. An examination of their records also showed that they usually secured around 62% of their quotes.

The factory needed $200K of business a month to make the owner a reasonable return, which meant they needed to be quoting about $325K a month. By watching this figure grow as the month unfolded, they were able to turn their focus toward or away from marketing. With a steady flow of quotes, these turned into enough work to keep the feeding buffer into the factory comfortably full. In turn, the periodic mayhem on the factory floor settled down and the whole business ran smoother.

Monitoring the dollar value of the quotes issued in the current month ensured that

1. next month the company would have enough quotes accepted;
2. the following month the factory would be working at its optimum and

3. the month after that, the bank account would be full.

The quotes were our lead indicator, and the bank balance our lag indicator.

David realized from our conversation that he needed an extra consulting session every two weeks to keep his feeding buffer topped up.

In effect, both David and the kitchen manufacturer had a tap they could turn up or down to ensure they had a feeding buffer that smoothed out the flow of work going through the bottleneck.

22

TIME TO COLLABORATE

Now it was time to collaborate. But not just any kind of collaboration.

This part of the puzzle is all about making sure the non-bottlenecks do as much bottleneck work as possible.

When you look closer and start asking, "Could anyone else do this task?" you'll be surprised at what you can delegate to others.

Remember, if non-bottlenecks have spare capacity, and it frees up bottleneck time, then it doesn't matter if they are slower at doing the job than the bottleneck.

Having set up enough idle, protective capacity around David, we needed to see if it was able to take some of his load.

I figured the easiest way for him to grasp the concept was for me to draw a picture.

23

THE ACCOUNTING STAFF

I used my own accounting practice to show how a job that flows through the business will need different skill levels at different points in the process.

In most cases a job-to-be-done will need some lower-skill work at the beginning (e.g., setup, onboarding), higher-skill work in the middle and some lower-skill tidy-up work at the end.

"In my accounting firm we obviously need our highly skilled accounting staff to be as productive as possible," I said. "It doesn't make sense for them to do the $20/hr tasks at the beginning of the job or the printing and binding at the end of the job.

"One of our biggest flow issues is having to pick up and put down jobs because information is missing. We now don't allow our skilled accounting staff to even pick up a job until an office junior has been through the information supplied by the client to make sure we have everything we need. The highly skilled staff therefore only take over when there's a good chance they'll be able to finish the job all in one go.

"While this didn't happen all the time, the results are significantly better than they used to be. The office junior now also does the lower-skill-level work to roll over last year's ledger, set up the job on the computer, load all the Tax Department information and scan all the other receipts and documents. He also does the end-point work of printing and binding up the final accounts."

I drew some red lines on the drawing and a couple of Xs to mark the part of the job that was non-bottleneck.

Over time our objective is to train the office juniors so they can move further and further toward the center, freeing up our experienced people to do even more of the higher-skill work in the middle.

The way to make sure that the junior staff can still do a great job is to have systems and procedures in place, and train them how to use them.

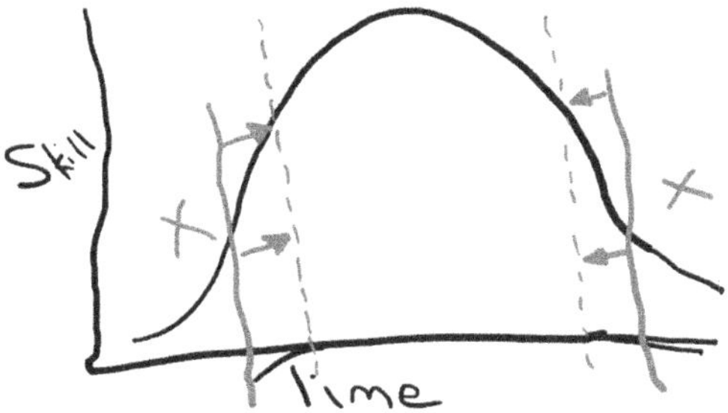

Another good example of the "collaborate" principle of delegating work to someone other than the bottleneck is to look at what should be happening in a restaurant kitchen.

Think of each meal as a mini project.

Should the highly skilled, highly paid chef take orders, peel the potatoes, clear tables and do the dishes? No!

The head chef cooks the steak to perfection, perfects the seasonings and sauces, and makes sure the presentation is up to snuff.

24

DAVID'S CLEVER IDEA

At an earlier meeting David had said that in the past some operations would slow down when the correct instruments weren't ready and laid out in the correct order. And the way he solved that problem was to lay them out himself.

I reminded him of this and asked, "So why aren't all the instruments laid out properly for you?"

"Some of the new staff don't know the procedures well or don't know my personal operating style. And so the wrong instrument will end up in the wrong place at times. I've found it's better if I just lay everything out myself. I know it doesn't make sense for me to be setting up or even checking my own instruments before each surgery, but I need a way to ensure it's done properly," said David.

He paused and thought about it for a few moments.

"Actually, there's no reason I can't take photos of my preferred instrument layout for each operation. We can laminate them and have them available for the staff to check."

"Anything else that interferes with your ability to get through operating procedures?" I asked.

"Looking at your graph, I'm starting to think that some of the post-operative recovery procedures and supervision could be done by someone else. Especially now that we've got spare nursing capacity. It would allow me to get back to the operating room faster and concentrate on doing the part in the middle that only I can do."

This was a great example of work previously being done by the bottleneck and now being offloaded to a non-bottleneck. And David was already thinking about how to take this a big step further.

25

MOLE MAPPING

I could tell David's business thinking was getting sharper because he started coming to me with light-bulb moments without any prompting on my part.

"I know I shouldn't be spending money on anything that doesn't keep me on the end of a scalpel," David began. "But I've got something else I want to run past you. It won't give me additional scalpel time, but I think it sort of makes sense anyway."

He went on to explain that a major risk with skin cancer is not detecting or treating it early enough. By using new technology and giving people regular scans to map the size and shape of their moles, they could pick up on pre-cancerous changes a lot earlier.

David and his team were thinking about buying an LED dermatoscope unit and using this new technology to offer mole mapping as a service. Now, our working rule had been *if it doesn't help the bottleneck, don't spend the money*. But this principle assumes that the bottleneck is always the limiting step for earning money.

The mole mapping technology was different because

non-bottleneck staff could be trained to run it and generate income without impacting David's time. As far as David being the bottleneck was concerned, this was free money!

David went for it. He bit the bullet and purchased the LED dermatoscope. And it ended up being a really good investment.

Not only did this move bring a great return, but because it could be run by non-bottleneck staff, the mole mapping service was effectively its own profit center: it was earning the business money without taking up any bottleneck time. For the first time ever, he could earn money while he was on vacation!

But it didn't stop there. Over time the mole mapping also sped up "scalpel time." By giving David an effective roadmap, it helped with planning and saved time when he had the patient under sedation.

"Are there any other ways you can make money without using your time?" I asked while we were on the subject.

"Well, we do sell various skin creams and lotions, but we've never really pushed it." He paused. "I think I might talk to the receptionist about moving the display to a better spot and pushing those sales a bit more."

These ideas were a departure from our mantra of just spending money on the bottleneck, so I just needed to check that he understood exactly where to spend his money.

"I just need to be clear that you still understand the things you won't be spending money on," I began.

"What do you mean?" asked David.

26

IT'S NOT ALWAYS THE BEST THING SINCE SLICED BREAD

"Let me tell you another story," I said to David. "Several years ago, when computerized phone systems were cutting-edge technology, I got a call from a salesperson who tried to get me to buy one for $30,000. I was confused! His sales pitch was that it would make my receptionist more efficient."

David and I had talked before about how in my accounting practice, the bottleneck was the highly qualified accounting staff who processed the work. The receptionist's job was, ultimately, to make sure the accounting staff were disturbed the least amount possible. Her role was to intercept phone calls, answer simple queries, collect papers coming in and return files to clients.

We really didn't mind if she was idle or "inefficient"—as long as she was *effective* at allowing the bottleneck staff to keep working.

And we really noticed the difference when she was away on vacation! All of a sudden, I was getting calls from people trying to sell me timeshares or memberships to a hotel chain. They'd looked up my name and pretended to know me, and now I was the one dealing with them. But they couldn't get past Laura when she was there!

After reminding David of this story, I said, "So while that fancy phone system may have made our receptionist more 'efficient,' the direct-dial function it came with would've meant more interruptions for our bottleneck staff! It would have actually slowed them down and made the whole business less efficient!

"The moral of the story is to know what your business bottleneck is. Until you figure that out and use that knowledge to make decisions, you'll continue to waste money on things that won't make a difference to your bottom line."

"Oh," said David. "Don't worry, I understand completely now that having idle staff is not a bad thing. As long as I'm busy," he clarified with a grin.

We quickly went through where he should be spending his money:

- Things that allow the bottleneck to increase the amount of time it is productive
- Things that increase the rate ($/minute) that the bottleneck earns money during its productive time
- Things that protect the bottleneck from being idle
- Things that earn money without consuming bottleneck capacity

27

CURATE

Now that David had finished offloading whatever tasks he could to the non-bottlenecks (i.e., collaborate), it was time to curate.

Curate what?

Curating is what a museum does. Only a fraction of its artifacts is on display at any one time. The curators decide which pieces will have the most impact on the visitors. It's a process of deciding what *not* to show to the public.

Deciding what not to offer to the public is also applicable in business.

In retail for example, shelf space is typically the bottleneck that limits how much money you can make. So the name of the game is to get as much margin per square foot as you can, usually with a combination of turning over high volumes of low-margin items and lower volumes of high-margin items.

In a bookshop, this can be done by selling a combination of greeting cards and high-end coffee table books (and of course, everything in between!).

Now, there are two things that absolutely kill retail.

The first is empty shelf space because fast sellers aren't restocked quickly enough. It's been said that the today's weather is the best predictor of tomorrow's weather. The same thinking needs to be applied to fast sellers. If it sold today, send off a replacement order that night. Don't wait for a large order to accumulate just so you can get free courier fees. The cost of the lost sale is far more than the saving!

The second retail killer is shelf space clogged up with slow/no sellers. These need to be curated and removed from the precious shelf space. That is, ruthlessly culling anything that is slowing the rate of money through the bottleneck.

In the same way, this phase for David was all about being selective with what passes through the precious bottleneck resource. It was time to decide what not to do!

28

GETTING RID OF THE RIFFRAFF

When it came to lifting David's income, it was obvious that tweaking prices and focusing on higher-value-per-minute procedures had helped. But we could still do more to lift the average.

He could

1. do fewer procedures that were slowing down throughput dollars and
2. stop seeing the types of patients who were slowing down throughput.

At our next meeting I asked David a simple question. "Who are your customers?"

"The patients I operate on," he answered.

"Do they come back more than once?"

"Not if I've done my job properly," he laughed.

"So who are your repeat customers, then?" I persisted.

He thought about it for a moment and then said, "I suppose it's the referring doctors."

"Do you ever get a referral from a particular doctor and you just *know* it's going to mean trouble for you?" I asked.

"Definitely! Birds of a feather and all that. Some of my doctors just seem to attract the ratbags. Patients miss appointments, don't follow up with post-op instructions—so there's often rework—and then they're usually the ones who don't pay anyway, so you end up having to chase them!"

I could feel his frustration. "So stop taking referrals from them," I said bluntly.

David looked confused. "Can you do that?" he asked.

"Why not? You have plenty of demand, so it's not like you need the work. Most of the time we're not talking about immediate life-and-death procedures, so it's not going to upset your oath to Hippocrates. And it's not as if these people don't have an alternative in town.

"It's no different than a factory. You need to have quality control done before the bottleneck. There's no point in putting something defective through the bottleneck and then throwing it out. You've just wasted precious bottleneck time."

Although I didn't mention it to David that day, I *have* recommended this to many clients over the years: Life is too short to deal with idiots. You can't afford to waste precious bottleneck time with them. Weed them out before they get to the bottleneck. You'll never know how much trouble you've saved yourself, but I promise you it's a great thing to do! Send the troublesome customers down the road to your competitors to slow them down and free yourself up. You'll be killing two birds with one stone!

To ensure his bottleneck capacity was not being wasted, David's next job was to tell his reception staff that whenever they received a referral from particular doctors, they were to say he was fully booked and recommend contacting another dermatologist.

David was expecting to get some pushback from his staff. Instead, the staff—who often suffered the brunt of managing disagreeable clients—were over the moon at this idea!

PART IV

THE GOODS: TAKEAWAYS AND "TLDR" BITS

29

SHOW ME THE MONEY!

At this point, we're going to leave David to it and let the numbers talk.

I'm also going to pause being a productivity flow expert and put my accountant's hat back on, because numbers are important. Without the numbers, you're just guessing.

As a friend of mine who's a top-notch winemaker once said to me, "You can make bad wine out of good grapes, but you can't make good wine out of bad grapes!" (He said it much more bluntly than that, but you get the drift!)

The same principle applies to business decisions. You can't make good decisions with bad numbers. Certainly, there are other, non-financial factors you need to take into account, but those usually need to come after you've done some work on the numbers. And they need to be the right numbers!

With the right numbers, you can answer questions like whether spending on additional assets or expenses will give you a good return on your money. Just like my decision *not* to spend $30,000 on a fancy phone system. And just like

David's decision to go ahead and spend $3,000 on more instruments. Both decisions (not to spend vs. to spend) were no-brainers when we thought about the effect they would have on profit.

Behind the scenes, David and I were constantly asking these number questions as his business evolved.

And the transformation had a massive impact on profit. The table below shows how the monthly profit grew as David implemented the steps we discussed.

	Patients per session	Average $ per op.	Number of sessions/month	Monthly Income	Mole map Income	Monthly Costs	Monthly Profit
Step 0	3	1000	18	54,000	-	45,000	9,000
Step 1	4	1000	18	72,000	-	45,000	27,000
Step 2	4	1500	18	108,000	-	45,000	63,000
Step 3	5	1500	18	135,000	5,000	50,000	90,000

1. Step 1: Fill up the bottleneck with work. Stop opening new operating lists until the existing ones are full. Have a stand-by list. Effect: Average goes from three procedures per operating list to four.
2. Step 2: Prioritize the higher $/minute work and increase prices on the low $/minute work. Effect: Average fee per procedure went from $1,000 to $1,500.
3. Step 3: Invest in more operating instruments, autoclaves, having an extra operating room nurse and the mole-mapping service. Effect: Average number of procedures per operating list went from four to five; mole-mapping income beginning to kick in.

Now, the figures on the table have been roughly rounded for the purposes of clarity. However, when you become aware of your bottleneck, then improvements in productivity of 30 to 50% are not uncommon. Going from three procedures per hour to four is a 33% productivity improvement.

You'll also remember that some of David's procedures were earning four times as much per minute as others. It wasn't difficult to add an average extra $500 to each procedure. When the extra productivity is combined with a shift to higher $/minute services *and* you have relatively high fixed expenses, then it's easy to see where this 10-fold increase in profit has come from.

But David saw a further doubling in profit once he increased his bottleneck capacity. He accomplished that not by working longer but by adding a new service and a really clever marketing strategy for his high-end, high $/minute services.*

Those extra steps did require some significant investment, both in time and money, but by that stage, David could afford it. But let's leave that for the moment and conclude with a quick summary of the FOCUS process.

***If you want to know what David's next moves were, you can find out in the bonus chapters available on my website. Download them for free at: www.grahamwscott.com/bonuschapters**

30

TOC NUGGETS

TOC Review

As I mentioned in my introductory remarks, David's journey followed the "Five Focusing Steps," the formalized recipe for implementing the Theory of Constraints (TOC) in an organization.

In his book *Rolling Rocks Downhill*, author and TOC expert Clarke Ching offers an easy-to-remember version of these steps called FOCUS or FOCCCUS:

- Find: identify the bottleneck
- Optimize: make sure the bottleneck is working at maximum capacity to improve overall output
- Coordinate, Collaborate, Curate: make sure everyone else (the non-bottlenecks) is working to improve the output of the bottleneck
- Upgrade: add more capacity to the bottleneck
- Start again: go back and check that something else hasn't become the bottleneck

One of the strengths of TOC thinking is that it focuses you on the one part of the operation that is the weakest link. This is the leverage point that will give you the most return on your time and effort.

Let's review the five FOCUS steps.

First, *find* the bottleneck.

Once you've found your bottleneck, your next step is to *optimize*—to make sure it's running at full capacity. I'm continually amazed at how much extra capacity is available, free of charge, when people start thinking about their bottleneck in these simple terms for the first time!

Next, fill that capacity and then look at the numbers to make sure that capacity is generating the most amount of income that it can.

Once the bottleneck is operating at full capacity, then everyone else around the bottleneck needs to be sure they are contributing to, and not sabotaging, the efforts at the bottleneck. *Coordinate* so that all the processes are working together. *Collaborate* so that any bottleneck work that can be done by a non-bottleneck is offloaded and everyone is working together to find better ways of doing it. And finally, *curate*, or offload any products, services or customers that are affecting the speed at which you make money.

This is the stage where some things will feel very counterintuitive. Like turning away business. Or realizing that after years of chasing productivity and efficiency, the only way a bottleneck can be kept busy is if there is idle, protective capacity around it. (As Jeremy found, his whole team runs better when some of the team members are idle.)

These first two steps (*Find* and *Optimize*) generally have little cost to the organization. It's all about uncovering hidden capacity. Step 3 (the three *Cs*) might cost a bit, but the return should make it a relative no-brainer.

Only after you have your bottleneck supported properly and running properly should you consider increasing the capacity of your bottleneck, which is Step 4.

And again, to find out how David tackled Step 4, download the bonus chapters for free at:

www.grahamwscott.com/bonuschapters

Lastly, it's important to revisit the first step, just in case the increased bottleneck capacity has caused another part of the process to become the weakest link. If it has, then address the new bottleneck. If not, then continue to recycle through the five steps as a process for ongoing improvement.

A common mistake people often make is to jump from Step 1 to Step 4. Just as it is a waste to put a turbocharger on a misfiring engine with a small fuel tank, it's a waste of money to add capacity to the bottleneck before it's using up its existing capacity and the protective capacity around it is in place. The expense of the turbocharger will be wasted.

And the beauty of Step 2 is that it's usually relatively cost effective. All you're doing is uncovering existing capacity. Adding extra capacity before you fix your wandering bottlenecks usually leads to disappointing results.

Of course, in real life the steps aren't always neat and linear. You tend to duck and dive between them—the key being that each change you make needs to give you the biggest bang as far as maximizing the dollars through the bottleneck.

David and I now revisit the steps most times we meet.

It has been a fascinating and fun journey of improvement and one that will end for David only when he retires. Last time we caught up, he pulled out some old financial accounts from when we first started working together. His business's taxable income now is 20 times higher than when we started.

In an hour doing multiple higher-value procedures with two operating rooms going, he can make twice what he was making from a single four-hour operating time back then. He has a lovely house and a second one at the beach, and his retirement is well and truly covered. A much better result than firing staff to keep the costs down!

Remember, we want an efficient bottleneck and effective non-bottlenecks. And in this case effective means keeping the bottleneck efficient even if it means having people and equipment idle!

As Debra Smith has said, "The Theory of Constraints can be summed up simply with two words: *focus and leverage.*"

31

THE MORAL OF THE STORY

In this book I refer to a lot of real-life business stories, day-to-day scenarios and analogies. Each one teaches a key business principle.

Rather than have you search through the book for a refresh on these lessons, I've put together a handy list of takeaways for each mini-story:

The old car

- A business can only go as fast as its slowest step.

The hospital porter

- Wandering bottlenecks are a sign you are not managing your true bottleneck.

Swim school

- Don't add capacity until the bottleneck is full.

The restaurants

- The speed at which you earn money matters.

The retail shop

- Know the daily cost of being open for business.

Driving to the airport

- Unpredictability + Buffer = Reliable Outcome

Diesel mechanics

- Mix up the big and small jobs.
- Not all jobs are urgent.
- Bring urgent work forward to fill gaps.
- Delay non-urgent work to create space.

Massage therapist

- Don't let lack of equipment hold up the bottleneck.

Software developer

- Protect the bottleneck by having idle capacity around it.

The gardening center

- Reduce the risk of a non-bottleneck breakdown.

Kitchen manufacturer

- Find the tap that smooths the flow of work into the bottleneck.

The accountant's office

- Keep your highly skilled people doing even more highly skilled work.

The computerized phone system

- Don't waste money making non-bottlenecks more efficient.

Mole mapping

- Income earned that doesn't touch the bottleneck is "free" money.

The bookshop

- Ruthlessly cull anything low value that consumes bottleneck capacity.

The numbers

- Without the right numbers, you're just guessing.

WHAT'S NEXT?

It should now be clear that you can apply the principles contained in this book to any organization with a bottleneck. And in reality, that includes all organizations. Farms, factories, service-based businesses, hotels, physical stores, e-commerce stores, restaurants, hospitals, not-for-profits, etc.

If you want to transform your own business by putting into practice some of the stuff that worked for David, then you've got a few options.

If you follow the principles outlined in the book, you can certainly go it alone.

Of course, if you're in a real hurry or want a guide, email me at **graham@grahamwscott.com** and let's discuss some one-on-one mentoring.

Running your own small business is tough, but it can be incredibly rewarding. Whatever approach you take to clear your bottleneck, I'd love to hear your success story!

ABOUT THE AUTHOR

Graham W. Scott (FCA, MCom) loves helping others solve gnarly business problems. It all started when he built his own accounting business from nothing. After growing it for 25 years, he planned his succession and sold it to an employee. Along the way, he has guided many other small business owners and organizations to squash obstacles, crank up profits and reclaim their "why." He thinks differently, and it works. When he's not crunching numbers or solving problems, Graham can be found enjoying the great outdoors in New Zealand with his family and friends.

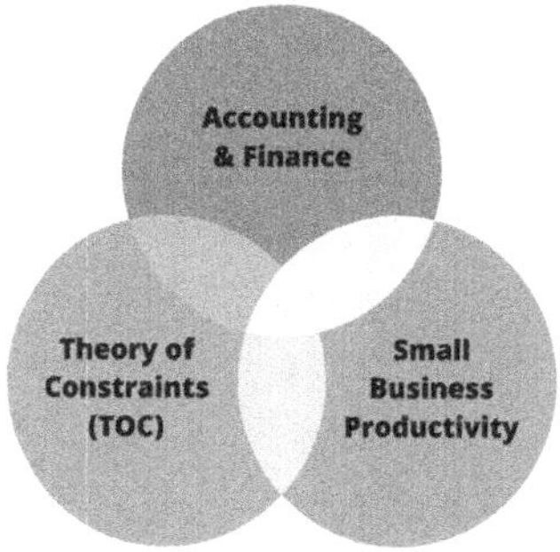

linkedin.com/in/grahamwscottnz